CONTENTS

S0-AWN-220

For pattern inquiries, please visit: www.go-crafty.com

PEEK-A-BOO blanket

YOU'LL NEED:

YARN (4)

Bernat® Baby Coordinates
(Solids: 5oz/140g)
(White: 5oz/140g)

A: Girl's Blanket
Main Color (MC)
48412 Sweet Pink - 2 balls
Contrast A
48420 Baby Pink - 2 balls
Contrast B
48320 Soft Mauve - 2 balls
Contrast C
48314 Orchid - 2 balls

B: Boy's Blanket
Main Color (MC)
48131 Blue BonBon - 2 balls
Contrast A
48128 Soft Blue - 2 balls
Contrast B
48738 Soft Turquoise - 2 balls
Contrast C
48005 White - 2 balls

HOOKS

Size I or 9 (5.5 mm) crochet hook *or size to obtain gauge*

MEASUREMENT

Approx 36" [91.5 cm] square.

GAUGE

12 sc and 13 rows = 4" [10 cm] with 2 strands held tog. *Take time to check gauge.*

INSTRUCTIONS

Note: Entire blanket is worked holding 2 strands of yarn tog.

Block 1 (make 9)
With 2 strands of MC, ch 17.
1st row: (RS). 1 sc in 2nd ch from hook. 1 sc in each ch to end of ch. Turn. 16 sc.
2nd row: Ch 1. 1 sc in each sc to end of row. Turn.
Rep last row until work from beg measures 5¼" [13 cm]. Fasten off at end of last row.

Edging
With RS facing, join 2 strands of A with sl st to any corner. Ch 1. Work in sc evenly around block, having 3 sc in each corner. Join with sl st to first sc. Fasten off.

Block 2 (make 9).
Work as for Block 1, substituting A for MC and MC for A.

Block 3 (make 9).
Work as for Block 1, substituting B for MC and C for A.

Block 4 (make 9).
Work as for Block 3, substituting C for B and B for C.

FINISHING

Sew blocks tog following diagram.

Border
Join 2 strands of MC with sl st in any corner st. Ch 1. 3 sc in same sp as sl st. Work in sc evenly around Blanket, having 3 sc in each corner. Join with sl st to first sc. Fasten off.

DIAGRAM

1	3	2	4	1	3
2	4	1	3	2	4
3	1	4	2	3	1
4	2	3	1	4	2
1	3	2	4	1	3
2	4	1	3	2	4

YOU'LL NEED:

YARN
Bernat® Baby Coordinates
(Solids: 5oz/140g)

Sizes: 6/9 (12/18) mos
48128 Soft Blue - 1 (1) ball

HOOKS
Size G or 6 (4 mm) crochet hook *or size to obtain gauge*

ADDITIONAL
4 buttons ½" [1.5 cm] in diameter.

SIZES
To fit baby's feet 6-9 (12-18) mos

GAUGE
16 sc and 18 rows = 4" [10 cm]. *Take time to check gauge.*

INSTRUCTIONS
Ch 9 (13).

1st rnd: 2 dc in 4th ch from hook (counts as 3 dc). 1 dc in each of next 4 (8) ch. 5 dc in last ch. Do not turn. Working into other side of foundation ch, work 2 dc in first ch. 1 dc in each of next 3 (7) ch. 5 dc in last ch. Join with sl st to top of ch-3. 22 (30) dc.

2nd rnd: Ch 2 (counts as hdc). 1 hdc in same sp as sl st. 2 hdc in next dc. 1 hdc in each of next 5 (10) dc. 2 hdc in each of next 5 dc. 1 hdc in each of next 6 (9) dc. 2 hdc in each of next 4 dc. 33 (41) dc.

3rd rnd: Ch 2 (counts as hdc). Working through back loops only, work 1 hdc in each st to end of rnd. Join with sl st to top of ch 2.

4th rnd: Ch 2 (counts as hdc). 1 hdc in each of next 11 (15) sts. (Yoh and draw up a loop in next st) twice. Yoh and draw through all loops on hook – hdc2tog made. 1 hdc in each of next 3 sts. Hdc2tog over next 2 sts. 1 hdc in each of next 14 (18) sts. Join with sl st to top of ch 2. 31 (39) sts.

5th rnd: Ch 2 (counts as hdc). 1 hdc in each of next 11 (15) sts. Hdc2tog over next 2 sts.

1 hdc in each of next 2 sts. Hdc2tog over next 2 sts. 1 hdc in each of next 13 (17) sts. Join with sl st to top of ch 2. 29 (37) sts.

6th rnd: Ch 1. Draw up a loop in each of next 2 sts. Yoh and draw through all loops on hook – sc2tog made. 1 sc in each of next 9 (14) sts. (Sc2tog over next 2 sts) 3 times. 1 sc in each of next 10 (13) sts. Sc2tog over last 2 sts. Join with sl st to first sc. 24 (32) sts.

7th rnd: Ch 1. 1 sc in each of next 10 (15) sts. (Sc2tog over next 2 sts) twice. 1 sc in each of next 10 (13) sc. Join with sl st to first sc. 22 (30) sts.

Size 6/9 mos only: Fasten off.
Size 12/18 mos only:
Next rnd: Ch 1. 1 sc in each of next 14 sc. (Sc2tog over next 2 sts) twice. 1 sc in each of next 12 sts. Join with sl st to first sc. Fasten off.

Strap (make 2)
Ch 9. 2 hdc in 3rd ch from hook. 1 hdc in each of next 5 ch. 6 hdc in last ch. Do not turn. Working into other side of foundation ch, work 1 hdc in each of next 5 ch. 4 hdc in last ch. Join with sl st to top of ch 2. Fasten off.

FINISHING
Note: Buttons are decorative only. Attach strap to front of Bootie as shown by sewing buttons through both thicknesses at each end of strap.

POLKA DOT blanket

YOU'LL NEED:

YARN
Bernat® Big Ball Baby Sport
(12¹/₃oz/350g)

Contrast A
21005 Baby White - 1 ball
Contrast B
21700 Tangerine- 1 ball

HOOKS
Size G or 6 (4 mm) crochet hook *or
size to obtain gauge*

MEASUREMENT
Approx 37" [94 cm] square.

GAUGE
16 dc and 9 rows = 4" [10 cm].
Each motif measures approx 7" [18 cm]
square. *Take time to check gauge.*

INSTRUCTIONS
Motif
Note: Ch 3 at beg of rnd counts as dc.
With Color 1, ch 4. Join with sl st in first ch
to form a ring.
1st rnd: Ch 3. 15 dc in ring. Join with sl st to
top of ch 3. Break Color 1. 16 dc.
2nd rnd: Join Color 2 with sl st in any sp
between 2 dc. Ch 3. 1 dc in same sp. 2 dc
in each sp between 2 dc around. Join with
sl st to top of ch 3. 32 dc.
3rd rnd: Ch 3. 1 dc in same sp as sl st. *1
dc in next dc. 2 dc in next dc. Rep from *

around to last dc. 1 dc in last dc. Join with
sl st to top of ch 3. 48 dc.
4th rnd: Ch 3. 1 dc in same sp as sl st. *1 dc
in each of next 3 dc. 2 dc in next dc. Rep
from * around to last 3 dc. 1 dc in each of
last 3 dc. Join with sl st to top of ch 3. Break
Color 2. 60 dc.
5th rnd: Join Color 1 with sl st to any dc.
Ch 4 (counts as tr). 2 dc in same sp. *Skip
next 2 dc. 1 hdc in each of next 2 dc. 1 sc
in each of next 6 dc. 1 hdc in each of next
2 dc. Skip next 2 dc.** (2 dc. 1 tr. Ch 2. 1 tr.
2 dc) in next dc (corner made). Rep from *
twice more, then from * to ** once. (2 dc. 1
tr) in same sp as first ch 4. Ch 2. Join with sl
st to top of ch 4.
6th rnd: Ch 3. *1 dc in each of next 2 dc.
1 dc in next hdc. 1 hdc in next hdc. 1 hdc
in next sc. 1 sc in each of next 4 sc. 1 hdc in
next sc. 1 hdc in next hdc. 1 dc in next hdc.
1 dc in each of next 2 dc. 1 dc in next tr.
(3 tr. Ch 2. 3 tr) in next corner ch-2 sp.**
1 dc in next tr. Rep from * twice more, then
from * to ** once. Join with sl st to top of
ch 3. Break Color 1.
7th rnd: Join Color 2 with sl
st in any corner ch-2 sp. Ch 2
(does not count as hdc).
(3 hdc. Ch 2. 3 hdc) in same
sp as sl st. *1 hdc in each st
across to next corner ch-2
sp.** (3 hdc. Ch 2. 3 hdc) in
corner ch-2 sp. Rep from *
twice more, then rep from

* to ** once. Join with sl st to top of ch 2.
Fasten off.
Make 12 Motifs having A as Color 1, and B
as Color 2.
Make 13 Motifs having B as Color 1, and A
as Color 2.

FINISHING
With B, join Motifs tog as shown in Diagram.
Edging
1st rnd: With RS facing, join A with sl st
in any corner ch-2 sp. Ch 1. Work 140 sc
evenly along each side edge, having 3 sc in
each corner. Join with sl st to first sc.
2nd rnd: Ch 1. 1 sc in each sc around, having 3 sc in each corner sc. Join B with sl st
to first sc.
3rd rnd: With B, *Sl st in each of next 3 sc.
(Sl st. Ch 3. 1 dc. Ch 3. Sl st) in next sc. Rep
from * around. Fasten off.

DIAGRAM

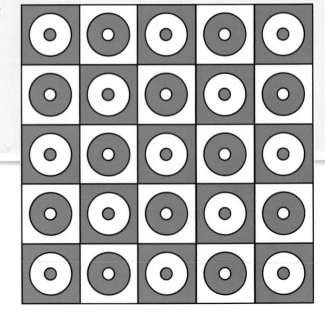

BIAS stripes blanket

MEASUREMENT
Approx 32" [81.5 cm] square.

GAUGE
16 dc and 9 rows = 4" [10 cm]. *Take time to check gauge.*

INSTRUCTIONS
Stripe Pat
With A, work 3 rows.
With B, work 3 rows.
With C, work 3 rows.
These 9 rows form Stripe Pat.

Blanket
Note: Skipped ch 3 at beg of each row counts as ch-3 sp.
With A, ch 6.
1st row: 1 dc in 4th ch from hook. 1 dc in each of next 2 ch. Turn.
2nd row: Ch 6. 1 dc in 4th ch from hook. 1 dc in each of next 2 ch – beg shell made. Skip next 3 dc. (Sl st. Ch 3. 3 dc) in next ch-3 sp – shell made. Turn. 2 shells.

3rd row: Beg shell. Skip next 3 dc. Shell in each of next 2 ch-3 sps. Join B. Turn. 3 shells.
4th row: With B, beg shell. Skip next 3 dc. Shell in each of next 3 ch-3 sps. Turn. 4 shells.
5th row: Beg shell. Skip next 3 dc. Shell in each of next 4 ch-3 sps. Turn. 5 shells.
6th row: Beg shell. Skip next 3 dc. Shell in each of next 5 ch-3 sps. Join C. Turn. 6 shells.
7th row: With C, beg shell. Skip next 3 dc. Shell in each ch-3 sp to end of row. Turn. 7 shells.
Keeping cont of Stripe Pat, rep last row 41 times more. 48 shells.
Proceed as follows
Next row: Ch 1. Sl st in each of next 3 dc and next ch-3 sp. Shell in same sp as last sl st. Shell in each ch-3 sp to last shell. Sl st in last ch-3 sp. Turn. 47 shells.
Keeping cont of Stripe Pat, rep last row until 2 shells rem.
Next row: Ch 1. Sl st in each of next 3 dc and next ch-3 sp. Shell in same sp as last sl st. Sl st in next ch-3 sp. Fasten off.

BUNNY buddy

YOU'LL NEED:

YARN 3
Bernat® Big Ball Baby Sport
(12¹/₃oz/350g)

Contrast A
21128 Baby Blue - 1 ball
Contrast B
21420 Baby Pink - 1 ball
Contrast C
21615 Baby Yellow - 1 ball

HOOKS
Size G or 6 (4 mm) crochet hook *or
size to obtain gauge*

ADDITIONAL
Stuffing.
Small quantity of black yarn for
embroidery.

MEASUREMENT
Approx 8" [20.5 cm] tall, excluding legs,
arms and ears.

GAUGE
16 sc and 17 rows = 4" [10 cm]. *Take time
to check gauge.*

INSTRUCTIONS
Body
With A, ch 2.
**1st rnd: 6 sc in 2nd ch from hook. Join
with sl st to first sc.
2nd rnd: Ch 1. 2 sc in each sc around. Join
with sl st to first sc. 12 sc.
3rd rnd: Ch 1. *1 sc in next sc. 2 sc in next
sc. Rep from * around. Join with sl st to first
sc. 18 sc.
4th rnd: Ch 1. *1 sc in each of next 2 sc. 2 sc

in next sc. Rep from * around. Join with sl
st to first sc. 24 sc.
5th rnd: Ch 1. *1 sc in each of next 3 sc. 2 sc
in next sc. Rep from * around. Join with sl
st to first sc. 30 sc.**
6th rnd: Ch 1. *1 sc in each of next 4 sc. 2 sc
in next sc. Rep from * around. Join with sl
st to first sc. 36 sc.
7th rnd: Ch 1. *1 sc in each of next 5 sc. 2 sc
in next sc. Rep from * around. Join with sl
st to first sc. 42 sc.
8th rnd: Ch 1. *1 sc in each of next 6 sc. 2 sc
in next sc. Rep from * around. Join with sl
st to first sc. 48 sc.
9th rnd: Ch 1. 1 sc in each sc around. Join
with sl st to first sc.
10th rnd: Ch 1. *1 sc in each of next 7 sc.
2 sc in next sc. Rep from * around. Join
with sl st to first sc. 54 sc.
11th rnd: As 9th rnd.
12th rnd: Ch 1. *1 sc in each of next 8 sc.
2 sc in next sc. Rep from * around. Join
with sl st to first sc. 60 sc.
13th rnd: As 9th rnd
14th rnd: Ch 1. *1 sc in each of next 9 sc.
2 sc in next sc. Rep from * around. Join
with sl st to first sc. 66 sc.
15th to 27th rnds: As 9th rnd.
28th rnd: Ch 1. *1 sc in each of next 9 sc.
Draw up a loop in each of next 2 sc. Yoh
and draw through 3 loops on hook
(sc2tog made). Rep from * around. Join
with sl st to first sc. 60 sts.
29th rnd: As 9th rnd.
30th rnd: Ch 1. *1 sc in each of next 8 sc.
Sc2tog. Rep from * around. Join with sl st
to first sc. 54 sts.

31st rnd: As 9th rnd.
32nd rnd: Ch 1. *1 sc in each of next 7 sc.
Sc2tog. Rep from * around. Join with sl st
to first sc. 48 sts.
33rd rnd: Ch 1. *1 sc in each of next 6 sc.
Sc2tog. Rep from * around. Join with sl st
to first sc. 42 sts.
34th rnd: Ch 1. *1 sc in each of next 5 sc.
Sc2tog. Rep from * around. Join with sl st
to first sc. 36 sts.
Stuff Body.
35th rnd: Ch 1. *1 sc in each of next 4 sc.
Sc2tog. Rep from * around. Join with sl st
to first sc. 30 sts.
36th rnd: Ch 1. *1 sc in each of next 3 sc.
Sc2tog. Rep from * around. Join with sl st
to first sc. 24 sts.
37th rnd: Ch 1. *1 sc in each of next 2 sc.
Sc2tog. Rep from * around. Join with sl st
to first sc. 18 sts.
38th rnd: Ch 1. *1 sc in next sc. Sc2tog. Rep
from * around. Join with sl st to first sc.
12 sts.
39th rnd: Ch 1. *Sc2tog. Rep from * around.
Join with sl st to first sc. 6 sts.
Break yarn, leaving a long end. Thread end
through rem sts and pull tightly. Fasten
securely.

Ears (make 2)
Stripe Pat
With A, work 3 rows.
With B, work 3 rows.
With C, work 3 rows.
These 9 rows form Stripe Pat.
Note: Skipped ch 3 at beg of each row
counts as ch-3 sp.

10

With A, ch 6.

1st row: 1 dc in 4th ch from hook. 1 dc in each of next 2 ch. Turn.

2nd row: Ch 6. 1 dc in 4th ch from hook. 1 dc in each of next 2 ch – beg shell made. Skip next 3 dc. (Sl st. Ch 3. 3 dc) in next ch-3 sp – shell made. Turn. 2 shells.

3rd row: Beg shell. Skip next 3 dc. Shell in each of next 2 ch-3 sps. Join B. Turn. 3 shells.

4th row: With B, beg shell. Skip next 3 dc. Shell in each of next 3 ch-3 sps. Turn. 4 shells.

5th row: Beg shell. Skip next 3 dc. Shell in each of next 4 ch-3 sps. Turn. 5 shells.

6th row: Beg shell. Skip next 3 dc. Shell in each of next 5 ch-3 sps. Join C. Turn. 6 shells.

7th row: With C, beg shell. Skip next 3 dc. Shell in each of next 6 ch-3 sps. Turn. 7 shells.

8th row: Beg shell. Skip next 3 dc. Shell in each of next 7 ch-3 sps. Turn. 8 shells.

9th row: Ch 1. Sl st in each of next 3 dc and next ch-3 sp. Beg shell in same sp as last sl st. Shell in each ch-3 sp to last shell. Join A with sl st in last ch-3 sp. Turn. 7 shells. Keeping cont of Stripe Pat, rep last row until 2 shells rem.

Next row: Ch 1. Sl st in each of next 3 dc and next ch-3 sp. Shell in same sp as last sl st. Sl st in next ch-3 sp. Fasten off.

Legs (make 2)

With B, ch 2.
Work from ** to ** as given for Body, joining A at end of 5th rnd.

6th rnd: With A, ch 1. 1 sc in each sc around. Join with sl st to first sc.

7th rnd: Ch 1. *1 sc in each of next 4 sc. Sc2tog. Rep from * around. Join with sl st to first sc. 25 sts.

8th to 10th rnds: As 6th rnd.

11th rnd: Ch 1. *1 sc in each of next 3 sc. Sc2tog. Rep from * around. Join with sl st to first sc. 20 sts.

12th to 16th rnds: As 6th rnd.
Fasten off. Stuff Legs lightly.

Arms (make 2)

With A, ch 15. Join with sl st to first ch to form ring, taking care not to twist ch.

1st rnd: Ch 1. 1 sc in each ch around. Join with sl st to first sc. 15 sc.

2nd to 12th rnds: Ch 1. 1 sc in each sc around. Join with sl st to first sc.

13th rnd: Ch 1. *2 sc in next sc. 1 sc in each of next 4 sc. Rep from * twice more. Join with sl st to first sc. 18 sc.

14th to 17th rnds: Ch 1. 1 sc in each sc around. Join with sl st to first sc.
Flatten work to align 9 sc on top of 9 sc.

Joining row: Working through both thicknesses of Arm, ch 1. Work 1 sc in each of next 9 sc. Turn.

Make 'Fingers'
1st 'Finger'

1st row: Ch 1. 1 sc in each of next 3 sc. Turn. Leave rem sts unworked.

2nd and 3rd rows: Ch 1. 1 sc in each sc across. Turn.

4th row: Ch 1. Draw up a loop in each of next 3 sc. Yoh and draw through all loops on hook – sc3tog made. Fasten off.

BUNNY buddy

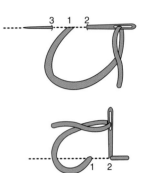

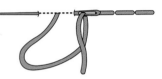

SATIN STITCH

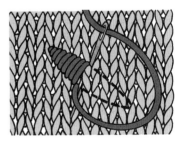

POM POM

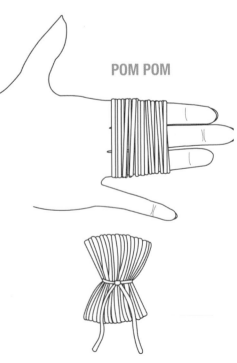

2nd and 3rd 'Finger': Work 1st to 4th rows as for 1st 'Finger'.
Stuff Arms lightly.

Nose
With B, ch 2.
1st rnd: 6 sc in 2nd ch from hook. Join with sl st to first sc.
2nd rnd: Ch 1. 1 sc in first sc. 2 sc in each of next 2 sc. 1 sc in next sc. 2 sc in each of next 2 sc. Join with sl st to first sc. 10 sc.
3rd rnd: Ch 1. 1 sc in each of first 2 sc. 2 sc in each of next 2 sc. 1 sc in each of next 3 sc. 2 sc in each of next 2 sc. 1 sc in last sc. Join with sl st to first sc. 14 sc.

4th rnd: Ch 1. 1 sc in each sc around. Join with sl st to first sc. Fasten off. Stuff Nose lightly.

Tail
Pom-pom: With C, wind yarn around 2 fingers approx 35 times. Remove from fingers and tie tightly in center. Cut through each side of loops. Trim to a smooth round shape.

FINISHING

Sew 2 sides of Ears tog meeting at corner to form cone shape. Sew Arms, Legs, Ears, Nose and Tail to Body. With B, embroider whiskers. With black yarn, embroider eyes using satin stitch and mouth using back stitch.

BABY blues blanket

YOU'LL NEED:

YARN ![4]

Bernat® Baby Coordinates
(5oz/140g)

48128 Soft Blue - 4 balls

HOOKS

Size I or 9 (5.5 mm) crochet hook *or
size to obtain gauge*

MEASUREMENTS
Approx 36" x 45" [91.5 x 114.5 cm].

GAUGE
13 sts and 14 rows = 4" [10 cm] in pattern.
Take time to check gauge.

INSTRUCTIONS
Note: Ch 3 at beg of row counts as dc.
Ch 113.

1st row: (RS). 1 dc in 4th ch from hook.
(counts as 2 dc). 1 dc in each ch to end of
ch. 111 dc. Turn.

2nd row: Ch 3. 1 dcfp around each of
next 2 dc. 1 dcbp around next dc. *1 dcfp
around each of next 3 dc. 1 dcbp around
next dc. Rep from * to last 3 dc. 1 dcfp
around each of next 2 dc. 1 dc in 2nd ch of
beg ch. Turn.

3rd row: Ch 3. 1 dc in each of next 2 sts. *1
dcfp around next st. 1 dc in each of next 3
sts. Rep from * to end of row, working last
dc in top of ch 3. Turn.

4th row: Ch 3. 1 dcfp around each of next 2
dc. 1 dcbp around next st. *1 dcfp around
each of next 3 dc. 1 dcbp around next st.
Rep from * to last 3 sts. 1 dcfp around each
of next 2 dc. 1 dc in top of ch 3. Turn.
Rep 3rd and 4th rows until Blanket measures approx 45"[114.5 cm], ending on a
4th row. Fasten off.

YOU'LL NEED:

YARN (4)
Bernat® Baby Coordinates
(Solids: 5oz/140g)

Note: Amounts are given for Set:
Dress and Bonnet or 1 ball for Bonnet
for each size.

Sizes 3 (6-12-18) mos
48420 Baby Pink - 1 (2-2-2) ball(s)

HOOKS
Size G or 6 (4 mm) crochet hook *or
size to obtain gauge*

ADDITIONAL
3 buttons for Dress
1 button for Bonnet.
1 yard [90 cm] of satin ribbon ½" [1.5
cm] wide.

SIZES
Dress
To fit chest measurement
3 mos   16" [40.5 cm]
6 mos   17" [43 cm]
12 mos 18" [45.5 cm]
18 mos 19" [48 cm]

Finished chest
3 mos   20" [51 cm]
6 mos   21" [53.5 cm]
12 mos 22" [56 cm]
18 mos 23½" [59.5 cm]

Bonnet
To fit baby size
3/6 (12/18) mos.

GAUGE
14 sts and 14 rows = 4" [10 cm] in Bodice
Pat. *Take time to check gauge.*

INSTRUCTIONS
The instructions are written for smallest
size. If changes are necessary for larger
sizes the instructions will be written thus
( ). When only one number is given, it applies to all sizes. For ease in working, circle
all numbers pertaining to your size.

DRESS
Back bodice
**Ch 36 (38-40-42).
***1st row: (RS). 1 sc in 2nd ch from hook.
1 sc in each ch to end of ch. Turn. 35 (37-
39-41) sc.
2nd row: Ch 1. 1 sc in each sc to end of
row. Turn.
3rd row: (Eyelet row). Ch 3 (counts as dc).
1 dc in next sc. *Ch 1. Skip next sc. 1 dc in
next sc. Rep from * to last sc. 1 dc in last sc.
Turn.
4th row: Ch 1. 1 sc in each of first 2 dc.
*1 dc in next ch-1 sp. 1 sc in next dc. Rep
from * to last dc. 1 sc in top of turning ch.
5th row: Ch 3 (counts as dc). *1 sc in next
dc. 1 dc in next sc. Rep from * to end of
row. Turn.
6th row: Ch 1. 1 sc in first dc. *1 dc in next
sc. 1 sc in next dc. Rep from * to end of
row. Turn.
Last 2 rows form pat.***

Shape armholes
1st row: (RS). Sl st in each of first 3 (4-4-4)
sts. Ch (1 or 3). Pat to last 2 (3-3-3) sts. Turn.
Leave rem sts unworked. 31 (31-33-35)
sts.**
Work 3 rows even in pat.

Divide for Back opening
Next row: Pat across next 15 (15-16-17) sts.
Turn. Leave rem sts unworked.
Cont on these 15 (15-16-17) sts until
armhole measures 4½ (5-5½-5¾)" [11.5
(12.5-14-14.5) cm], ending with a WS row.
Fasten off.

With RS of work facing, skip next st. Join
yarn with sl st in next st. Ch 1. Pat to end of
row. 15 (15-16-17) sts.
Cont even in pat until armhole measures
4½ (5-5½-5¾)" [11.5 (12.5-14-14.5) cm],
ending with a WS row. Fasten off.

Skirt
Join yarn with sl st to first ch of foundation
ch of Back Bodice.

1st row: Ch 1. 1 sc in each of first 1 (0-1-0)
ch. *2 sc in next ch. 1 sc in each of next 3
ch. Rep from * to last 2 (1-2-1) ch. 2 (1-1-2)
sc in next ch. 1 sc in each of last 1 (0-1-0)
ch. 44 (46-48-52) sc.
2nd row: Ch 3 (counts as dc). *2 dc in next
sc. (1 dc. Ch 3. 1 sc) in next sc. Rep from *
to last sc. 1 dc in last sc. Turn.
3rd row: Ch 1. 1 sc in first dc. *(3 dc. Ch 3. 1
sc) in next ch-3 sp. Rep from * to last dc. 1
dc in top of turning ch. Turn.
Rep last 2 rows of Skirt Pat until Skirt measures 9¼(10½-12-13¾)"[23.5 (26.5-30.5-35)
cm], ending with a WS row. Fasten off.

Front bodice
Work from ** to ** as given for Back Bodice.
Cont even in pat until armhole measures 8
rows less than Back Bodice.
31 (31-33-35) sts.

Shape neck
1st row: (RS). Pat across next 10 (10-11-11)
sts. Yoh and draw up a loop in each of next
2 sts. Yoh and draw through all loops on
hook – hdc2tog made. Turn. Leave rem sts
unworked.
2nd row: Ch 2. Hdc2tog over first 2 sts. Pat
to end of row. Turn.
3rd row: Ch 2. Pat to last 2 sts. Hdc2tog
over last 2 sts. Turn. 8 (8-9-9) sts rem.
4th row: As 2nd row.
Work 4 rows even in pat. Fasten off.

With RS of work facing, skip next 7 (7-7-9)
sts. Join yarn with sl st to rem sts: Ch 2.
Hdc2tog over same st as sl st and next st.
Pat to end of row. Turn.
2nd row: Ch 2. Pat to last 2 sts. Hdc2tog
over last 2 sts. Turn.
3rd row: Ch 2. Hdc2tog over first 2 sts. Pat
to end of row. Turn.
4th row: As 2nd row.
Work 4 rows even in pat. Fasten off.

Skirt
Work as given for Back Bodice Skirt.

15

Sleeves

Ch 22 (26-28-30).

Work from *** to *** as given for Back Bodice. 21 (25-27-29) sts after 1st row.

Next row: Ch 1. (1 sc. 1 dc) in first sc. *1 sc in next dc. 1 dc in next sc. Rep from * to last 2 sts. 1 sc in next dc. (1 dc. 1 sc) in last sc. Turn.

Next row: Ch 3 (counts as dc). *1 sc in next dc. 1 dc in next sc. Rep from * to end of row. Turn.

Next row: Ch 1. 1 sc in first dc. *1 dc in next sc. 1 sc in next dc. Rep from * to end of row. Turn.

Rep last 3 rows 4 (4-5-5) times more. 31 (35-39-41) sts.

Cont even in pat until work from beg measures 5¼ (6½-7½-8)" [13 (16.5-19-20.5) cm], ending with a WS row. Fasten off.

Cuff

Join yarn with sl st to first ch of foundation ch of Sleeve.

1st row: Ch 1. 1 sc in each of first 0 (0-2-0) ch. *2 sc in next ch. 1 sc in each of next 3 ch. Rep from * to last ch. 1 (2-2-1) sc in last ch. 26 (32-34-36) sc.

****2nd row:** Ch 3 (counts as dc). *2 dc in next sc. (1 dc. Ch 3. 1 sc) in next sc. Rep from * to last sc. 1 dc in last sc. Turn.

3rd and 4th rows: Ch 1. 1 sc in first dc. *(3 dc. Ch 3. 1 sc) in next ch-3 sp. Rep from * to last dc. 1 dc in top of turning ch. Turn. Fasten off.****

FINISHING

Pin garment pieces to measurements. Cover with a damp cloth, leaving cloth to dry.

Sew shoulder seams.
Place marker at each side of sleeve ¾" (1-1-1)" [2 (2.5-2.5-2.5) cm] down from top edge. Sew in sleeves, placing rows above markers along unworked sts on front and back left for armholes. Sew side and sleeve seams.

Collar

With RS of work facing, join yarn with sl st to top corner of left back. Ch 1. Work 48 (48-52-58) sc around neck edge to next corner.

Work from **** to **** as given for Cuffs.

Back edging and button loops

Place markers on right back opening for button loops, having top loop at top corner, bottom loop 1" [2.5 cm] up from bottom of back opening and rem loop spaced evenly between.

Join yarn with sl st to right top of back opening. Ch 1. 1 sc in same sp as sl st. (Ch 4. Work in sc to next button loop marker) 3 times. Work in sc to bottom of back opening and up along opposite side of back opening. Fasten off.

Sew buttons to correspond to button loops. Thread ribbon through eyelet row of Bodice.

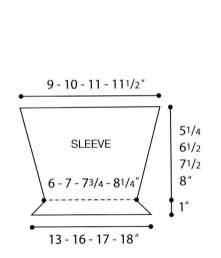

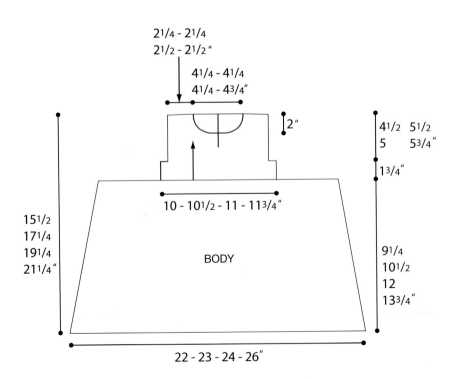

BONNET

Ch 2.

1st rnd: 6 sc in 2nd ch from hook. Join with sl st to first sc.

2nd and 3rd rnds: Ch 1. 2 sc in each sc around. Join with sl st to first sc. 24 sc at end of 3rd rnd.

4th rnd: Ch 1. *1 sc in each of next 3 sc. 2 sc in next sc. Rep from * around. Join with sl st to first sc. 30 sc.

5th and alt rnds: Ch 1. 1 sc in each sc around. Join with sl st to first sc.

6th rnd: Ch 1. *1 sc in each of next 4 sc. 2 sc in next sc. Rep from * around. Join with sl st to first sc. 36 sc.

8th rnd: Ch 1. *1 sc in each of next 5 sc. 2 sc in next sc. Rep from * around. Join with sl st to first sc. 42 sc.

10th rnd: Ch 1. *1 sc in each of next 6 sc. 2 sc in next sc. Rep from * around. Join with sl st to first sc. 48 sc.

11th rnd: As 5th rnd.

Size 12/18 mos only

12th rnd: Ch 1.
*1 sc in each of next 7 sc. 2 sc in next sc. Rep from * around. Join with sl st to first sc. 54 sc.

13th rnd: As 5th row.

14th rnd: Ch 1. *1 sc in each of next 8 sc. 2 sc in next sc. Rep from * around. Join with sl st to first sc. 60 sc.

15th rnd: Ch 1. 1 sc in each sc around. Join with sl st to first sc.

Both sizes

1st row: Ch 3 (counts as dc). *2 dc in next sc. (1 dc. Ch 3. 1 sc) in next sc. Skip next 2 sc. Rep from * to last 3 sc. 1 dc in next sc. Turn. Leave rem 2 sts unworked. Working back and forth in rows, proceed as follows:

2nd row: Ch 1. 1 sc in first dc. *(3 dc. Ch 3. 1 sc) in next ch-3 sp. Rep from * to last st. 1 dc in last st. Turn.

Rep last row for pat until work from marked row measures approx 2¾ (3¾)" [7 (9.5) cm], ending with a RS row. Do not fasten off.

Neck and chin band

Ch 1. Work 42 sc along side edges of bonnet. Ch 17. Turn.

2nd row: Ch 1. 1 sc in 2nd ch from hook. 1 sc in each of next 15 ch. 1 sc in each sc to end of row. Turn.

3rd row: (Buttonhole row). Ch 1. 1 sc in each sc to last 4 sc. Ch 2. Skip next 2 sc. 1 sc in each of last 2 sc. Turn.

4th row: Ch 1. 1 sc in each sc to end of row, working 2 sc in ch-2 sp. Fasten off

Sew button to correspond to buttonhole.

CASCADING ripples blanket

YOU'LL NEED:

YARN
Bernat® Baby Coordinates
(Solids: 5oz/140g)
(White: 5oz/140g)
(Ombres: 4¼oz /120g)

Main Color (MC)
48131 Blue BonBon - 1 ball
Contrast A
49744 Funny Prints - 2 balls
Contrast B
48128 Soft Blue - 3 balls
Contrast C
48005 White - 1 ball

HOOKS
Size I or 9 (5.5 mm) crochet hook *or size to obtain gauge*

MEASUREMENT
Approx 36"[91.5 cm] square.

GAUGE
12 sc and 13 rows = 4"[10 cm] with 2 strands tog. *Take time to check gauge.*

STITCH GLOSSARY
Cascading Ripple Pat
With MC, work 1 row.
With A, work 1 row.
Rep last 2 rows once more.
With B, work 1 row.
With A, work 1 row.
Rep last 2 rows twice more.
With B, work 1 row.
With C, work 1 row.
Rep last 2 rows 3 times more.
With B, work 1 row.
With A, work 1 row.
Rep last 2 rows twice more.
These 24 rows form Cascading Ripple Pat.

INSTRUCTIONS
Note: Entire blanket is worked holding 2 strands of yarn tog.
First and last sc of each row is left un-worked.

With 2 strands of MC, ch 167. Mark every 50th ch for easier counting.

1st row: 1 sc in 2nd ch from hook. *(Ch 1. Skip next ch. 1 sc in next ch) 6 times. Ch 2. (1 sc in next ch. Ch 1. Skip next ch) 6 times. 1 sc in next ch.** Skip next 2 ch. 1 sc in next ch. Rep from * 4 times more, then from * to ** once more. Fasten off. Turn. 166 sts.

2nd row: Join 2 strands of A, with sl st to first ch-1 sp. Ch 1. 1 sc in same sp as sl st. (Ch 1. Skip next sc. 1 sc in next ch-1 sp) 5 times. Ch 1. *(1 sc. Ch 2. 1 sc) in next ch-2 sp. (Ch 1. Skip next sc. 1 sc in next ch-1 sp) 6 times. **Skip next 2 sc. (1 sc in next ch-1 sp. Ch 1. Skip next sc) 6 times. Rep from * 4 times more, then from * to ** once more. Fasten off. Turn.
First 2 rows of Cascading Ripple Pat are complete.
Keeping cont of Cascading Ripple Pat, rep last row until Cascading Ripple Pat has been worked 4 times.
With MC, work 1 row. With A, work 1 row. With MC, work 1 row. Do not turn.

Edging
With 2 strands of MC, working along side edge of Blanket, proceed as follows: Ch 1. 1 sc in side of each sc down side of blanket. Fasten off.
Join 2 strands of MC with sl st to first sc on other side of Blanket. Ch 1. 1 sc in side of each sc up side of Blanket. Fasten off.

SHELL STITCH blanket

MEASUREMENTS
Approx 34" x 40" [86.5 x 101.5 cm].

GAUGE
14 dc and 8 rows = 4" [10 cm]. *Take time
to check gauge.*

INSTRUCTIONS
Note: Ch 3 at beg of rnd counts as dc
throughout.

Beg at center, with A, ch 24.
1st rnd: [1 dc. (Ch 2. 2 dc) 3 times] all in 4th
ch from hook. *Skip next 3 ch. (2 dc. Ch 2.
2 dc) in next ch – shell made. Rep from * to
last ch. (Shell. Ch 2. Shell) in last ch. Working across opposite side of ch, **skip next
3 ch. Shell in next ch (where previous shell
was worked). Rep from ** across. Join with
sl st to top of ch 3. Break A.
2nd rnd: Join B with sl st in next ch-2 sp.
Ch 3. 1 dc. Ch 2. 2 dc in same sp – beg
shell made. (Ch 2. Shell) in same sp. Skip
next ch-2 sp. (Shell. Ch 2. Shell) in next
corner ch-2 sp. *Shell in next ch-2 sp. Rep
from * to next corner ch-2 sp. (Shell. Ch
2. Shell) in next corner ch-2 sp. Skip next
ch-2 sp. (Shell. Ch 2. Shell) in next corner
ch-2 sp. **Shell in next ch-2 sp. Rep from
** across. Join with sl st to top of ch 3.
3rd rnd: Sl st in next dc and next ch-2 sp.
Beg shell in same ch-2 sp. *Shell in next
ch-2 sp. Rep from * around. Join with sl st
to top of ch 3. Break B.
4th rnd: Join A with sl st in next ch-2 sp.
Beg shell in same ch-2 sp. (Shell. Ch 2.
Shell) in next corner ch-2 sp. *Shell in
each ch-2 sp to next corner. (Shell. Ch 2.
Shell) in next corner ch-2 sp. Rep from *
twice more. **Shell in next ch-2 sp. Rep
from ** across. Join with sl st to top of ch
3. Break A.

5th rnd: Join C with sl st in any corner ch-2
sp. Beg shell in same sp. *Shell in next
ch-2 sp. Rep from * around. Join with sl st
to top of ch 3. Break C.
6th rnd: Join A with sl st in any corner
ch-2 sp. (Beg shell. Ch 2. Shell) in same
ch-2 sp. *Shell in each ch-2 sp to next
corner. (Shell. Ch 2. Shell) in next corner
ch-2 sp. Rep from * twice more. **Shell in
next ch-2 sp. Rep from ** across. Join with
sl st to top of ch 3. Break A.
7th rnd: With B, as 5th rnd. Do not break B.
8th rnd: Sl st in next dc and next ch-2
sp. (Beg shell. Ch 2. Shell) in same ch-2
sp. *Shell in each ch-2 sp to next corner.
(Shell. Ch 2. Shell) in next corner ch-2 sp.
Rep from * twice more. **Shell in next
ch-2 sp. Rep from ** across. Join with sl st
to top of ch 3. Break B.
9th rnd: Join A with sl st in next ch-2 sp.
Beg shell in same ch-2 sp. *Shell in next
ch-2 sp. Rep from * across. Join with sl st
to top of ch 3. Break A.
10th rnd: Join C with sl st in any corner
ch-2 sp. (Beg shell. Ch 2. Shell) in same
ch-2 sp. *Shell in each ch-2 sp to next
corner. (Shell. Ch 2. Shell) in next corner
ch-2 sp. Rep from * twice more. **Shell in
next ch-2 sp. Rep from ** across. Join with
sl st to top of ch 3. Break C.
11th rnd: As 9th rnd.
12th rnd: Join B with sl st in any corner
ch-2 sp. (Beg shell. Ch 2. Shell) in same
ch-2 sp. *Shell in each ch-2 sp to next
corner. (Shell. Ch 2. Shell) in next corner
ch-2 sp. Rep from * twice more. **Shell in
next ch-2 sp. Rep from ** across. Join with
sl st to top of ch 3.
13th rnd: Sl st in next dc and next ch-2 sp.
Beg shell in same ch-2 sp. *Shell in next
ch-2 sp. Rep from * around. Join with sl st
to top of ch 3. Break B.
Rep 4th to 13th rnds for pat until work
measures approx 34"[86.5 cm] wide, ending on a 6th or 11th rnd of pat. Fasten off.

BLUEmeanie toy

MEASUREMENT
Approx 7½" [19 cm] tall, excluding legs,
arms and horns.

GAUGE
16 sc and 17 rows = 4" [10 cm]. *Take time
to check gauge.*

INSTRUCTIONS

Monster Body
With A, ch 2.
**1st rnd: 6 sc in 2nd ch from hook. Join
with sl st to first sc.
2nd rnd: Ch 1. 2 sc in each sc around. Join
with sl st to first sc. 12 sc.
3rd rnd: Ch 1. *1 sc in next sc. 2 sc in next
sc. Rep from * around. Join with sl st to first
sc. 18 sc.
4th rnd: Ch 1. *1 sc in each of next 2 sc. 2 sc
in next sc. Rep from * around. Join with sl
st to first sc. 24 sc.
5th rnd: Ch 1. *1 sc in each of next 3 sc. 2 sc
in next sc. Rep from * around. Join with sl

st to first sc. 30 sc.**
6th rnd: Ch 1. *1 sc in each of next 4 sc. 2 sc
in next sc. Rep from * around. Join with sl
st to first sc. 36 sc.
7th rnd: Ch 1. *1 sc in each of next 5 sc. 2 sc
in next sc. Rep from * around. Join with sl
st to first sc. 42 sc.
8th rnd: Ch 1. *1 sc in each of next 6 sc. 2 sc
in next sc. Rep from * around. Join with sl
st to first sc. 48 sc.
9th rnd: Ch 1. 1 sc in each sc around. Join
with sl st to first sc.
10th rnd: Ch 1. *1 sc in each of next 7 sc.
2 sc in next sc. Rep from * around. Join
with sl st to first sc. 54 sc.
11th rnd: As 9th rnd.
12th rnd: Ch 1. *1 sc in each of next 8 sc.
2 sc in next sc. Rep from * around. Join
with sl st to first sc. 60 sc.
13th rnd: As 9th rnd.
14th rnd: Ch 1. *1 sc in each of next 9 sc.
2 sc in next sc. Rep from * around. Join
with sl st to first sc. 66 sc.
15th to 27th rnds: As 9th rnd.
28th rnd: Ch 1. *1 sc in each of next 9 sc.
Draw up a loop in each of next 2 sc. Yoh
and draw through all 3 loops on hook –
sc2tog made. Rep from * around. Join with
sl st to first sc. 60 sts.
29th rnd: As 9th rnd.
30th rnd: Ch 1. *1 sc in each of next 8 sc.
Sc2tog. Rep from * around. Join with sl st
to first sc. 54 sts.
31st rnd: As 9th rnd.
32nd rnd: Ch 1. *1 sc in each of next 7 sc.
Sc2tog. Rep from * around. Join with sl st
to first sc. 48 sts.
33rd rnd: Ch 1. *1 sc in each of next 6 sc.
Sc2tog. Rep from * around. Join with sl st
to first sc. 42 sts.
34th rnd: Ch 1. *1 sc in each of next 5 sc.

Sc2tog. Rep from * around. Join with sl st
to first sc. 36 sts.
Stuff Body.
35th rnd: Ch 1. *1 sc in each of next 4 sc.
Sc2tog. Rep from * around. Join with sl st
to first sc. 30 sts.
36th rnd: Ch 1. *1 sc in each of next 3 sc.
Sc2tog. Rep from * around. Join with sl st
to first sc. 24 sts.
37th rnd: Ch 1. *1 sc in each of next 2 sc.
Sc2tog. Rep from * around. Join with sl st
to first sc. 18 sts.
38th rnd: Ch 1. *1 sc in next sc. Sc2tog. Rep
from * around. Join with sl st to first sc.
12 sts.
39th rnd: Ch 1. *Sc2tog. Rep from * around.
Join with sl st to first sc. 6 sts.
Break yarn, leaving a long end. Complete
stuffing Body. Thread end through rem sts
and pull tightly. Fasten securely.

Legs (make 2)
With C, ch 2.
Work from ** to ** as given for Body, joining B at end of 5th rnd.
6th rnd: With B, ch 1. 1 sc in each sc
around. Join with sl st to first sc.
7th rnd: Ch 1. *1 sc in each of next 4 sc.
Sc2tog. Rep from * around. Join with sl st
to first sc. 25 sts.
8th to 10th rnds: As 6th rnd. Join A with sl
st at end of 10th rnd.
11th rnd: With A, ch 1. *1 sc in each of next
3 sc. Sc2tog. Rep from * around. Join with
sl st to first sc. 20 sts.
12th rnd: With A, as 6th rnd. Join B with sl
st at end of rnd.
13th and 14th rnds: As 6th rnd. Join A with
sl st at end of 14th rnd.
15th and 16th rnds: With A, as 6th rnd.
Fasten off. Stuff Leg lightly.

Arms (make 2)

With A, ch 15. Join with sl st to first ch to form ring, taking care not to twist ch.

1st rnd: Ch 1. 1 sc in each ch around. Join with sl st to first sc. 15 sc.

2nd rnd: Ch 1. 1 sc in each sc around. Join B with sl st to first sc.

3rd and 4th rnds: With B, as 2nd rnd. Join A with sl st at end of 4th rnd.

5th and 6th rnds: With A, as 2nd rnd. Join B with sl st at end of 6th rnd.

7th to 10th rnds: As 3rd to 6th rnds.

11th and 12th rnds: As 3rd and 4th rnds. Join C with sl st at end of 12th rnd.

13th rnd: With C, ch 1. *2 sc in next sc. 1 sc in each of next 4 sc. Rep from * twice more. Join with sl st to first sc. 18 sc.

14th to 17th rnds: Ch 1. 1 sc in each around. Join with sl st to first sc. Flatten work to align 9 sc on top of 9 sc.

Joining row: Working through both thicknesses of Arm, ch 1. Work 1 sc in each of next 9 sc. Turn.

Make 'Claws':

1st 'Claw': 1st row: Ch 1. 1 sc in each of next 3 sc. Turn. Leave rem sts unworked.

2nd row: Ch 1. 1 sc in each sc across. Join A. Turn.

3rd row: With A, ch 1. 1 sc in each sc across. Turn.

4th row: Ch 1. Draw up a loop in each of next 3 sc. Yoh and draw through all loops on hook – sc3tog made. Fasten off.

2nd and 3rd 'Claws': Work 1st to 4th rows as for 1st 'Claw'.
Stuff Arm lightly.

Horns (make 2)

With A, ch 2.

1st rnd: 4 sc in 2nd ch from hook. Join with sl st to first sc.

2nd rnd: Ch 1. 2 sc in each sc around. Join with sl st to first sc. 8 sc.

3rd to 6th rnds: Ch 1. 1 sc in each around. Join with sl st to first sc. Fasten off at end of 6th rnd.

FINISHING

Sew Arms, Legs and Horns in position to Body as shown in picture. With white yarn, embroider eyes using satin stitch. With B, make straight stitches in center of each eye. With 2 strands of white yarn, make a chain 6" [15 cm] long for mouth. Fasten off. Sew mouth in position as shown in picture. With white yarn, embroider 'fangs' using satin stitch.

STRAIGHT STITCH

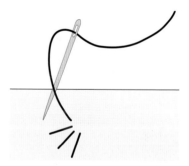

SATIN STITCH

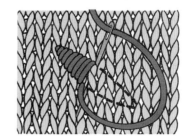

HOODED blanket

MEASUREMENT
Approx 30" [76 cm] square.

GAUGE
14 dc and 7 rows = 4"[10 cm]. *Take time to check gauge.*

STITCH GLOSSARY
Trbp: (Yo) twice and draw up a loop around post of next st at back of work, inserting hook from right to left. (Yo and draw through 2 loops on hook) 3 times—1 trbp made.
Trfp: (Yo) twice and draw up a loop around post of next st at front of work, inserting hook from right to left. (Yo and draw through 2 loops on hook) 3 times—1 trfp made.

INSTRUCTIONS
Ch 106.
Foundation row: (WS). 1 sc in 2nd ch from hook. 1 sc in each ch to end of ch. 105 sc. Turn.
2nd row: Ch 3 (counts as dc). 1 trfp in next sc. *1 trbp in each of next 5 sc. 1 trfp in next st. Rep from * to last sc. 1 dc in last sc. Turn.
3rd row: Ch 3 (counts as dc). 1 trfp in next st. *1 dc in each of next 5 dc. 1 trfp in next st. Rep from * to last st. 1 dc in top of turning ch. Turn.
4th row: Ch 3 (counts as dc). 1 trbp in next st. *1 dc in each of next 5 dc. 1 trbp in next st. Rep from * to last st. 1 dc in top of turning ch. Turn.
5th row: As 3rd row.
6th row: Ch 3 (counts as dc).1 trbp in next st. *1 trbp in each of next 5 dc. 1 trbp in next st. Rep from * to last st. 1 dc in top of turning ch. Turn.
Rep 3rd to 6th rows for Waffle pat until work from beg measures 29½" [75 cm], ending with RS facing for next row.
Next row: Ch 1. 1 sc in each st to end of row. Fasten off.

Hood
Ch 4.
1st row: (RS). 4 dc in 4th ch from hook. Turn. 5 dc.
2nd row: Ch 3 (counts as dc). 1 dc in first dc (counts as 2 dc). 1 dc in each of next 3 dc. 2 dc in top of turning ch. Turn. 7 dc.
3rd row: Ch 3. 1 dc in first dc (counts as 2 dc). 1 dc in each of next 2 dc. 2 dc in next dc. 1 dc in each of next 2 dc. 2 dc in top of turning ch. Turn. 10 dc.
4th row: Ch 3. 1 dc in first dc (counts as 2 dc). (1 dc in each of next 2 dc. 2 dc in next dc) twice. 1 dc in each of next 2 dc. 2 dc in top of turning ch. Turn. 14 dc.
5th row: Ch 3. 1 dc in first dc (counts as 2 dc). 1 dc in each of next 3 dc. 2 dc in next dc. 1 dc in each of next 4 dc. 2 dc in next dc. 1 dc in each of next 3 dc. 2 dc in top of turning ch. Turn. 18 dc.
6th row: Ch 3. 1 dc in first dc (counts as 2 dc). 1 dc in each dc to last st. 2 dc in top of turning ch. Turn. 20 dc.
7th row: Ch 3. 1 dc in first dc (counts as 2 dc). 1 dc in each of next 6 dc. 2 dc in next dc. 1 dc in each of next 4 dc. 2 dc in next dc. 1 dc in each of next 6 dc. 2 dc in top of turning ch. Turn. 24 dc.
8th row: As 6th row. 26 dc.
9th row: Ch 3. 1 dc in first dc (counts as 2 dc). (1 dc in each of next 4 dc. 2 dc in next dc) 5 times. Turn. 32 dc.
10th row: As 6th row. 34 dc.
11th row: Ch 3. 1 dc in first dc (counts as 2 dc). (1 dc in each of next 10 dc. 2 dc in next dc) 3 times. Turn. 38 dc.
12th and 13th rows: As 6th row twice. 42 dc.
14th row: Ch 3. 1 dc in first dc (counts as 2 dc). 1 dc in each of next 8 dc. (2 dc in next dc. 1 dc in each of next 7 dc) 4 times. 2 dc in top of turning ch. Turn. 48 dc.
15th row: As 6th row. 50 dc. Do not turn.
16th row: (RS). Ch 1. Working from left to right instead of right to left as usual, work 1 reverse sc in each dc across. Fasten off.
Pin Hood to upper left corner of Blanket.

FINISHING
Edging
1st rnd: With RS of work facing, join MC with sl st to upper right corner of Blanket. Ch 1. (3 sc in corner. work 69 sc across side of Blanket) 4 times, working through both thicknesses to join Hood to Blanket where they meet. Join with sl st to first sc.
2nd rnd: Ch 1. Working from left to right instead of from right to left as usual, work 1 reverse sc in each sc around. Join with sl st to first sc. Fasten off.

SINGLE CROCHET diaper bag

YOU'LL NEED:

YARN 🔵4

Bernat® Baby Coordinates
(Solids: 5oz/140g)
(White: 5oz/140g)

A: Girl's Bag
Main Color (MC)
48412 Sweet Pink - 2 balls
Contrast A
48420 Baby Pink - 1 ball
Contrast B
48320 Soft Mauve - 1 ball
Contrast C
48314 Orchid - 1 ball

B: Boy's Bag
Main Color (MC)
48131 Blue BonBon - 2 balls
Contrast A
48128 Soft Blue - 1 ball
Contrast B
48738 Soft Turquoise - 1 ball
Contrast C
48005 White - 1 ball

HOOKS
Size I or 9 (5.5 mm) crochet hook *or size to obtain gauge*

ADDITIONAL
2 buttons
Plastic canvas 15" x 6" [38 x 15 cm]

MEASUREMENTS
Approx 15" x 12" x 6" [38 x 30.5 x 15 cm].

GAUGE
12 sc and 13 rows = 4" [10 cm] with 2 strands tog. *Take time to check gauge.*

INSTRUCTIONS

Note: Entire bag is worked holding 2 strands of yarn tog.

Block 1 (make 18).
With 2 strands of MC, ch 8.
1st row: 1 sc in 2nd ch from hook. 1 sc in each ch to end of ch. Turn. 7 sc.
2nd to 7th rows: Ch 1. 1 sc in each sc across. Turn. Fasten off at end of 7th row.

Edging
With RS facing, join A with sl st to any corner. Ch 1. Work in sc evenly around block, having 3 sc in each corner. Join with sl st to first sc. Fasten off.

Block 2 (make 18).
Work as for Block 1, substituting A for MC and MC for A.

Block 3 (make 20).
Work as for Block 1, substituting B for MC and C for A.

Block 4 (make 20).
Work as for Block 3, substituting C for B and B for C.

FINISHING
Sew blocks tog for Front, Back, Top, Bottom and Sides, following diagrams.
Sew Front, Back, Sides and Bottom into a Bag.
Sew Top to Back only, leaving 3 sides open.

Opening Edging
With RS facing, join MC with sl st in any st at open section of top. Ch 1. 1 sc in every sc around opening, having 3 sc in outer corners. Join with sl st to first sc. Fasten off.

Insert plastic canvas sheet in bottom of bag.

Handles (make 2).
With 2 strands of MC, ch 80.
1st row: 1 sc in 2nd ch from hook. 1 sc in each ch to end of ch. 79 sc.
2nd row: Ch 1. 1 sc in each sc to end of row. Turn.
Rep last row 3 times more. Fasten off. Sew handles to sides of bag as shown in picture.

Button loops (make 2).
With 2 strands of MC, ch 15.
1st row: 1 sc in 2nd ch from hook and each ch to end of ch. Fasten off.
Fold loops in half and sew to front of Top 1½ blocks in from each side edge. Sew buttons to Front to correspond to button loops.

SIDES

1	4	1	4
2	3	2	3

TOP AND BOTTOM

4	1	4	1	4
3	2	3	2	3

FRONT AND BACK

1	4	1	4	1
2	3	2	3	2
3	2	3	2	3
4	1	4	1	4

FANTASY flowers pullover

YOU'LL NEED:

YARN 3
Bernat® Softee Baby
(Solids:5oz/140g)
(Ombre: 4¼oz/120g)

All Sizes
Main Color (MC)
30207 Rumba Rose - 1 ball
Contrast A
30205 Prettiest Pink - 1 ball
Contrast B
31415 Candy Baby - 1 ball

HOOKS
Size G or 6 (4 mm) crochet hook *or size to obtain gauge*

ADDITIONAL
3 buttons

SIZES
To fit chest measurement
6 mos 17" [43 cm]
12 mos 18" [45.5 cm]
18 mos 19" [48 cm]
2 yrs 21" [53.5 cm]

Finished chest
6 mos 20" [51 cm]
12 mos 21" [53.5 cm]
18 mos 22" [56 cm]
2 yrs 24" [61 cm]

GAUGE
17 sc and 18 rows = 4" [10 cm]. *Take time to check gauge.*

INSTRUCTIONS
The instructions are written for smallest size. If changes are necessary for larger sizes the instructions will be written thus ( ). When only one number is given, it applies to all sizes. For ease in working, circle all numbers pertaining to your size.

Note: Each color has its own pattern stitch. When color change occurs, pattern stitch also changes.

Back
**With MC, ch 44 (46-48-52).

Foundation row: 1 sc in 2nd ch from hook and in each ch to end of ch. Turn. 43 (45-47-51) sts.
1st row: Ch 1. 1 sc in first sc. *1 sc in back loop of next st. 1 sc in front loop of next st. Rep from * to last 2 sts. 1 sc in back loop of next st. 1 sc in both loops of last st. Turn. Rep last row 10 times more. Join B at end of last row.
Next row: With B, ch 1. 1 sc in first sc. *Ch 1. Skip next sc. 1 sc in next sc. Rep from * to end of row. Turn.
Next row: Ch 1. 1 sc in first sc. 1 sc in next ch-1 sp. *Ch 1. Skip next sc. 1 sc in next ch-1 sp. Rep from * to last sc. 1 sc in last sc. Turn.
Next row: Ch 1. 1 sc in first st. *Ch 1. Skip next sc. 1 sc in next ch-1 sp. Rep from * to last 2 sc. Ch 1. Skip next sc. 1 sc in last st. Turn.
Rep last 2 rows until work from beg measures 6¼ (7-7½-8)" [16 (18-19-20.5) cm], ending with WS row. Break B.

Shape armholes
With RS of work facing, skip first 5 (5-5-6) sts. Join A with sl st in next ch-1 sp. Ch 1. 1 sc in same sp as sl st. *1 dc in next st. 1 sc in next st. Rep from * to last 5 (5-5-6) sts. Turn. Leave rem sts unworked. 33 (35-37-39) sts.
2nd row: Ch 3 (counts as dc). Skip first sc. *1 sc in next dc. 1 dc in next sc. Rep from * to end of row. Turn.
3rd row: Ch 1. *1 dc in next sc. 1 sc in next dc. Rep from * across. Turn.**
Rep last 2 rows 6 (7-8-8) times more, then 2nd row once. Fasten off.

Front
Work from ** to ** as given for Back.
Rep last 2 rows 2 (3-3-3) times more, then 2nd row once.

Shape neck: (RS). Pat across first 9 (10-11-12) sts. *(Yo and draw up a loop in next st) twice. Yo and draw through all loops on hook – Hdc2tog made. Turn. Leave rem sts unworked.

Next row: Pat across. Turn.
Next row: Pat to last 2 sts. Hdc2tog over last 2 sts. Turn.
Rep last 2 rows twice more. 7 (8-9-10) sts. Work 1 (1-3-3) row(s) even in pat. Fasten off.
With RS facing, skip next 11 sts of first row of neck shaping. Join A with sl st in next st. Ch 2 (does not count as st). Hdc2tog over first 2 sts. Pat to end of row. 10 (11-12-13) sts.
Next row: Pat across. Turn.
Next row: Hdc2tog over first 2 sts. Pat to end of row. Turn.
Rep last 2 rows twice more. 7 (8-9-10) sts. Work 1 (1-3-3) row(s) even in pat. Fasten off.

Sleeves
With B, ch 30 (32-34-36).
Foundation row: (RS). 1 sc in 2nd ch from hook. *Ch 1. Skip next ch. 1 sc in next ch. Rep from * to end of ch. Turn. 29 (31-33-35) sts.
1st row: Ch 1. 1 sc in first sc. *1 sc in next ch-1 sp. Ch 1. Skip next sc. Rep from * to last ch-1 sp and sc. 1 sc in next ch-1 sp. 1 sc in last sc. Turn.
2nd row: Ch 1. 1 sc in first sc. *Ch 1. Skip next sc. 1 sc in next ch-1 sp. Rep from * to last 2 sc. Ch 1. Skip next sc. 1 sc in last sc. Turn.
3rd row: As 1st row.
4th row: (Inc row). Ch 1. 2 sc in first sc. Ch 1. Skip next sc. 1 sc in next ch-1 sp. *Ch 1. Skip next sc. 1 sc in next ch-1 sp. Rep from * to last sc. Ch 1. 2 sc in last sc. Turn. 31 (33-35-37) sts.
5th row: Ch 1. 1 sc in each sc and ch-1 sp across. Join A. Turn.
6th row: With A, ch 1. 1 sc in first sc. *1 dc in next sc. 1 sc in next sc. Rep from * to end of row. Turn.
7th row: Ch 3 (counts as dc). *1 sc in next dc. 1 dc in next sc. Rep from * to end of row. Turn.
8th row: (Inc row). Ch 3 (counts as dc). 1 sc in first dc. *1 dc in next sc. 1 sc in next dc. Rep from * to last dc. (1 sc. 1 dc) in last dc. Turn. 33 (35-37-39) sts.

9th row: Ch 1. 1 sc in first dc. *1 dc in next sc. 1 sc in next dc. Rep from * to end of row. Turn.

10th row: As 7th row.

11th row: As 9th row. Join MC. Turn.

12th row: (Inc row). With MC, ch 1. 2 sc in first sc. *1 sc in back loop only of next dc. 1 sc in front loop only of next sc. Rep from * to last dc. 2 sc in both loops of last dc. Turn. 35 (37-39-41) sc.

13th to 15th rows: Ch 1. 1 sc in first sc. *1 sc in front loop only of next sc. 1 sc in back loop only of next sc. Rep from * to last 2 sc. 1 sc in front loop only of next sc. 1 sc in both loops of last sc. Turn.

16th row: (Inc row). Ch 1. 2 sc in first sc. *1 sc in front loop only of next sc. 1 sc in back loop only of next sc. Rep from * to last 2 sc. 1 sc in front loop only of next sc. 2 sc in both loops of last sc. Turn. 37 (39-41-43) sts.

17th row: Ch 1. 1 sc in first sc. *1 sc in back loop only of next sc. 1 sc in front loop only of next sc. Rep from * to last sc. 1 sc in both loops of last sc. Turn. Join B. These 2nd to 17th rows form Stripe Texture Pat.

Cont in Stripe Texture Pat, working 2 sts at each end of every following 4th row from previous inc to 39 (43-47-47) sts, taking inc sts into pat.

Work even in pat until sleeve from beg measures 6½ (7½-8-8½)" [16.5 (19-20.5-21.5) cm]. Place markers at each end of last row.

Work 5 (5-5-7) rows more in pat. Fasten off.

Flower (make 3)

With B, ch 6. Join with sl st to first ch to form ring.

1st rnd: Ch 1. 12 sc in ring. Join with sl st to first sc.

2nd rnd: Ch 1. *(1 sc. 1 dc) in next sc. (1 dc. 1 sc) in next sc. Rep from * around. Join with sl st to first sc. Fasten off.

FINISHING

Pin garment pieces to measurements and cover with damp cloth, leaving cloth to dry.

Sew right shoulder only. Sew sleeves in armholes, placing rows above markers to skipped sts of armholes to form square armholes. Sew 3 Flowers evenly spaced across MC band at bottom of Front. Sew side and sleeve seams.

Neck edging and button loops

1st row: With RS of work facing, join A with sl st to right corner of left shoulder. 1 sc in each of first 3 (3-2-3) sts of left front shoulder. *Ch 3 (button loop). 1 sc in each of next 2 (2-3-3) sts. Rep from * once more. Ch 3 (button loop). 1 sc in next corner st. 12 sc down left front neck edge. 1 sc in each of next 11 sts across front neck edge. 12 sc up right front neck edge. 1 sc in each st across back and left shoulder to end of row. Do not turn.

2nd row: Working from left to right instead of right to left as usual, work 1 reverse sc in each sc, ending at corner of left front neck edge. Fasten off. Sew buttons to back left shoulder to correspond to button loops.

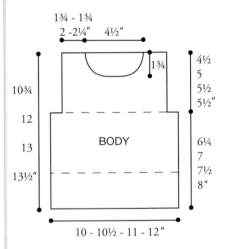

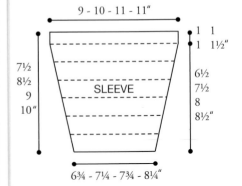

FANTASY flowers jacket

YOU'LL NEED:

YARN
Bernat® Softee Baby
(Solids: 5oz/140g)
(Ombre: 4¼oz/120g)

All Sizes
Main Color (MC)
30207 Rumba Rose - 1 ball
Contrast A
02001 Pink - 1 ball
Contrast B
30205 Prettiest Pink - 1 ball
Contrast C
31415 Candy Baby - 1 ball

HOOKS
Size G or 6 (4 mm) crochet hook *or
size to obtain gauge*

ADDITIONAL
2 buttons

SIZES

To fit chest measurement

6 mos	17"	[43 cm]
12 mos	18"	[45.5 cm]
18 mos	19"	[48 cm]
2 yrs	21"	[53.5 cm]

Finished chest

6 mos	21"	[53.5 cm]
12 mos	22"	[56 cm]
18 mos	23"	[58.5 cm]
2 yrs	25"	[63.5 cm]

GAUGE

17 sts and 13 rows = 4" [10 cm] in pat. *Take
time to check gauge.*

INSTRUCTIONS

The instructions are written for smallest
size. If changes are necessary for larger
sizes the instructions will be written thus
( ). When only one number is given, it applies to all sizes. For ease in working, circle
all numbers pertaining to your size.

Note: To change color, work to last 2 loops
on hook. Draw loop of next color through
2 loops on hook to complete st and proceed in next color.

Back

With MC, ch 47 (49-51-55).
Foundation row: (RS). *Insert hook in 3rd ch
from hook. Yo and draw up a loop. Yo and
draw through one loop on hook. Yo and
draw through 2 loops on hook – Exsc made.
1 exsc in each ch to end of ch. Turn. 45
(47-49-53) sts.*
1st row: Ch 1. 1 exsc in each st across. Turn.
Rep last row for Pat until work from beg
measures 6¼ (6¾-7½-8)"[16 (17-19-20.5)
cm], ending with a WS row. Fasten off.

Shape armholes

With RS facing, skip first 6 (6-6-7) sts. Join
MC with sl st in next st. Ch 1. 1 exsc in
same st as last sl st. 1 exsc in each st to last
6 (6-6-7) sts. Turn. Leave rem sts unworked.
33 (35-37-39) sts.
Cont even in pat until work from beg measures 11 (11½-12½-13½)" [28 (29-32-34.5)
cm]. Fasten off.

Left front

**With MC, ch 34
(36-38-42).
Foundation row:
(RS). 1 exsc in 3rd ch
from hook. 1 exsc
in each ch to end of
ch. Turn. 32 (34-36-
40) sts.
Work in pat as given
for Back until 14
(14-16-16) rows are
completed.**
Next row: (But-
tonhole row). Ch
1. 1 exsc in each st
to last 3 sts. Ch 1.
Skip next st. 1 exsc
in each of last 2 sts.
Turn.

Next row: Ch 1. 1 exsc in each of next 2 sts.
1 exsc in next ch-1 sp. 1 exsc in each st to
end of row. Turn.

Shape front

Next row: Ch 1. 1 exsc in each st to last 2
sts. *(Insert hook in next st. Yo and draw up a
loop. Yo and draw through 1 loop on hook
twice. Yo and draw through all loops on
hook)*– Exsc2tog made. Turn. 31 (33-35-39)
sts.
Next row: Ch 1. Exsc2tog over first 2 sts. 1
exsc in each st across. Turn.
Rep last 2 rows until piece measures same
length as Back to armhole. Fasten off.

Shape armhole

Next row: (RS). Skip first 6 (6-6-7) sts. Join
MC with sl st in next st. Ch 1. 1 exsc in
same sp as last sl st. 1 exsc in each st to last
2 sts. Exsc2tog over last 2 sts. Turn.
Next row: Ch 1. Exsc2tog over first 2 sts. 1
exsc in each st across. Turn.
Next row: Ch 1. 1 exsc in each st to last 2

sts. Exsc2tog over last 2 sts. Turn.
Rep last 2 rows until 10 (10-11-12) sts rem.
Next row: Ch 1. 1 exsc in each st across. Turn.
Rep last row of Pat until work measures same length as Back to shoulder, ending with a WS row. Fasten off.

Right front
Work from ** to ** as given for Left Front.
Next row: (Buttonhole row). Ch 1. 1 exsc in each of first 2 sts. Ch 1. Skip next st. 1 exsc in each st to end of row. Turn.
Next row: Ch 1. 1 exsc in each st to last 3 sts. 1 exsc in next ch-1 sp. 1 exsc in each of last 2 sts. Turn.

Shape front
Next row: Ch 1. Exsc2tog over first 2 sts. 1 exsc in each st to end of row. Turn. 31 (33-35-39) sts.
Next row: Ch 1. 1 exsc in each st to last 2 sts. Exsc2tog over last 2 sts. Turn.
Rep last 2 rows until work from beg measures same length as Back to armhole.

Shape armhole
Next row: (RS). Ch 1. Exsc2tog over first 2 sts. 1 exsc in each st to last 6 (6-6-7) sts. Turn. Leave rem sts unworked.
Next row: Ch 1. 1 exsc in each st to last 2 sts. Exsc-2tog over last 2 sts. Turn.
Next row: Ch 1. Exsc2tog

FANTASY flowers jacket

over first 2 sts. 1 exsc in each st across. Turn.

Rep last 2 rows until 10 (10-11-12) sts rem.

Next row: Ch 1. 1 exsc in each st across. Turn. Rep last row of Pat until work measures same length as Back to shoulder, ending with a WS row. Fasten off.

Sleeves

Note: To change color, work to last 2 loops on hook. Draw loop of next color through 2 loops on hook to complete st and proceed in next color.

With MC, ch 31 (31-33-33).

Foundation row: (RS). 1 exsc in 3rd ch from hook and in each ch to end of ch. Turn. 29 (29-31-31) sts.

2nd row: Ch 1. 1 exsc in each st to end of row. Turn.

3rd row: Ch 1. 2 exsc in first st. 1 exsc in each st to last st. 2 exsc in last st. Turn.

4th row: As 2nd row. Join A.

5th row: With A, as 3rd row.

6th to 8th rows: As 2nd row three times. Join B at end of 8th row.

9th to 12th rows: With B, as 5th to 8th rows. Join C at end of 12th row.

13th to 16th rows: With C, as 5th to 8th rows. Join MC at end of 16th row. These 5th to 16th rows form Stripe Pat.

Cont in pat, keeping cont of Stripe Pat and work 2 exsc at each end of next and every following alt row to 41 (41-43-47) sts. Work even in pat until sleeve from beg measures 8 (9-9½-10)" [20 .5 (23-24-25.5) cm], ending with a WS row. Fasten off.

Flower

Note: Ch 2 at beg of rnd does not count as st.

With C, ch 3.

1st rnd: 6 hdc in 3rd ch from hook. Join with sl st to first hdc. 6 hdc.

2nd rnd: Ch 2. 2 hdc in back loop of each hdc around. Join with sl st to back loop of first hdc.

3rd rnd: As 2nd rnd. Join with sl st to both loops of first hdc. 24 hdc.

Sizes 6 and 12 mos only:

4th rnd: Ch 1. 1 sc in same sp as sl st. *Ch 5. Skip next 3 hdc. 1 sc in next hdc. Rep from * to last 3 hdc. Ch 5. Skip last 3 hdc. Join with sl st to first sc.

5th rnd: (Petals). Ch 1. *(1 sc. 1 hdc. 3 dc. 1 hdc. 1 sc) in next ch-5 sp. Rep from * around. Join with sl st to first sc. Fasten off.

Sizes 18 mos and 2 yrs only:

4th rnd: Ch 1. *Working in back loops only 1 hdc in next hdc. 2 hdc in next hdc. Rep from * around. Join with sl st to back loop of first hdc. 36 hdc.

5th rnd: Ch 1. 1 sc in same sp as sl st. *Ch 6. Skip next 5 hdc. 1 sc in next hdc. Rep from * around. Join with sl st to first sc.

6th rnd: (Petals). Ch 1. *(1 sc. 1 hdc. 1 dc. 3 tr. 1 dc. 1 hdc. 1 sc) in next ch-6 sp. Rep from * around. Join with sl st to first sc. Fasten off.

FINISHING

Pin garment pieces to measurements and cover with damp cloth, leaving cloth to dry.

Sew shoulder seams. Place markers on each side of sleeves 1½" [4 cm] down from top edge. Sew sleeves in armholes, placing rows above markers to skipped sts of armholes to form square armholes. Sew side and sleeve seams. Sew button to WS of right front and RS of left front to correspond to buttonholes. Sew Flower to center of right front leaving petals free.

Edging

With RS facing, join MC with sl st to bottom corner of right front. Ch 1. Work sc evenly up right front edge to beg of neck shaping. 2 sc in corner. Work sc evenly up right front neck, across back neck and down left front neck to front edge. 2 sc in corner. Work sc evenly to bottom left front corner. Fasten off.

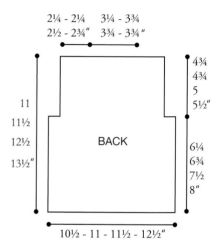

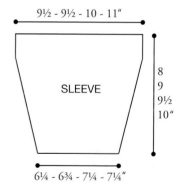

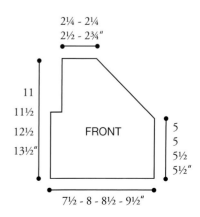

FANTASY FLOWERS
Hat And Scarf

SIZES

Hat
To fit child's head 6-12 mos (18 mos-2 yrs)

Scarf
Approx 5" x 42" [12.5 x 106.5 cm].

GAUGE

17 sc and 18 rows = 4" [10 cm]. *Take time to check gauge.*

INSTRUCTIONS

The instructions are written for smallest size. If changes are necessary for largest size the instructions will be written thus ( ). When only one number is given, it applies to both sizes. For ease in working, circle all numbers pertaining to your size.

Hat

With MC, ch 3.
1st rnd: 8 hdc in 3rd ch from hook. Join with sl st to first hdc. 8 hdc.
2nd rnd: Ch 2 (does not count as st). Working in back loops only, 2 hdc in each hdc around. Join with sl st to back loop of first hdc.

3rd rnd: As 2nd rnd. 32 hdc.
4th rnd: Ch 2 (does not count as st). * Working in back loops only, 2 hdc in next hdc. 1 hdc in next hdc. Rep from * around. Join with sl st to back loop of first hdc. 48 hdc.
5th rnd: Ch 2 (does not count as st). Working in back loops only, 1 hdc in each hdc around. Join with sl st to back loop of first hdc.
6th rnd: Ch 2 (does not count as st). *Working in back loops only, 1 hdc in each of next 3 hdc. 2 hdc in next hdc. Rep from * around. Join with sl st to back loop of first hdc. 60 hdc.
7th rnd: Ch 2 (does not count as st). Working in back loops only, 1 hdc in each hdc around. Join with sl st to back loop of first hdc.
Size 6-12 mos only: Rep last rnd until work from beg measures 5"[12.5 cm]. Join A at end of last rnd.
With A, rep last rnd twice more. Fasten off.
Size 18 mos-2 yrs only: 8th rnd: Ch 2 (does not count as st). Working in back loops only, 1 hdc in each hdc around. Join with sl st to back loop of first hdc.
9th rnd: Ch 2 (does not count as st). *Working in back loops only, 1 hdc in each of next 4 hdc. 2 hdc in next hdc. Rep from * around. Join with sl st to back loop of first hdc. 72 hdc.
Rep 8th rnd until work from beg measures 6"[15 cm]. Join A at end of last rnd.
With A, rep 8th rnd twice more. Fasten off.
Both sizes: Flower: Join A with sl st in rem front loop of any stitch of 4th rnd.
1st rnd: Ch 1. 1 sc in same sp as sl st. *Working in rem loops only, ch 6. Skip next 5 sts. 1 sc in next st. Rep from * to last 5 sts. Ch 6. Skip last 5 sts. Join with sl st to first sc.
2nd rnd: (Petals). Ch 1. *(1 sc. 1 hdc. 5 dc. 1 hdc. 1 sc) all in next ch-6 sp. Rep from * around. Join with sl st to first sc. Fasten off.

Scarf

With MC, ch 23.
Foundation row: (RS). 1 dc in 4th ch from hook (counts as 2 dc). 1 dc in each ch to end of ch. Turn. 21 dc.
1st row: Ch 2 (counts as dc). 1 dc in each dc to end of row. Turn.
Rep last row 8 times more. Join A at end of last row.
With A, rep last row twice more. Join MC at end of last row.
With MC, rep last row 4 times more. Join A at end of last row.
Rep last 6 rows of Stripe Pat until work from beg measures approx 36"[91.5 cm], ending with 2 rows of A. Join MC at end of last row.
With MC, rep last row 10 times more. Fasten off.

Flower (make 2)

With A, ch 3.
1st rnd: 6 hdc in 3rd ch from hook. Join with sl st to first hdc. 6 hdc.
2nd rnd: Ch 2 (does not count as st). 2 hdc in each hdc around. Join with sl st to first hdc.
3rd rnd: As 2nd rnd. 24 hdc.
4th rnd: Ch 1. 1 sc in same sp as sl st. *Ch 5. Skip next 3 hdc. 1 sc in next hdc. Rep from * to last 3 hdc. Ch 5. Skip last 3 hdc. Join with sl st to first sc.
5th rnd: (Petals). Ch 1. *(1 sc. 1 hdc. 3 dc. 1 hdc. 1 sc) all in next ch-5 sp. Rep from * around. Join with sl st to first sc. Fasten off.

Sew one Flower to MC section at each end of scarf.

FANTASY flowers bunny

YOU'LL NEED:

YARN ③
Bernat® Softee Baby
(Solids: 5oz/140g)
(Ombre: 4¼oz/120g)

Main Color (MC)
30207 Rumba Rose - 1 ball
Contrast A
02001 Pink - 1 ball
Contrast B
30205 Prettiest Pink - 1 ball
Contrast C
31415 Candy Baby- 1 ball

HOOKS
Size G or 6 (4 mm) crochet hook *or size to obtain gauge*

ADDITIONAL
2 buttons

MEASUREMENTS
Approx 10" [25.5 cm] high.

GAUGE
17 sc and 18 rows = 4" [10 cm]. *Take time to check gauge.*

INSTRUCTIONS
Base: With MC, ch 2.
1st rnd: 6 sc in 2nd ch from hook. Join with sl st to first sc. 6 sc.
2nd rnd: Ch 1. 2 sc in each sc around. Join with sl st to first sc. 12 sc.
3rd rnd: Ch 1. *1 sc in next sc. 2 sc in next sc. Rep from * around. Join with sl st to first sc. 18 sc.
4th rnd: Ch 1. *1 sc in each of next 2 sc. 2 sc in next sc. Rep from * around. Join with sl st to first sc. 24 sc.
5th rnd: Ch 1. *1 sc in each of next 3 sc. 2 sc in next sc. Rep from * around. Join with sl st to first sc. 30 sc.
6th rnd: Ch 1. *1 sc in each of next 4 sc. 2 sc in next sc. Rep from * around. Join with sl st to first sc. 36 sc.

Body
1st rnd: Ch 1. 1 sc in back loop only of each sc around. Join with sl st to first sc. 36 sc.
2nd rnd: Ch 1. *1 sc in each of next 5 sc. 2 sc in next sc. Rep from * to end of rnd. Join with sl st to first sc. 42 sc.
3rd rnd: Ch 1. 1 sc in each sc around. Join with sl st to first sc.
4th rnd: As 2nd rnd. 49 sc.
5th to 26th rnds: Ch 1. 1 sc in each sc around. Join with sl st to first sc.
27th rnd: (Dec rnd). Ch 1. 1 sc in each of first 5 sc. *Draw up a loop in each of next 2 sc. Yo and draw through all 3 loops on hook - Sc2tog made.* *1 sc in each of next 5 sc. Sc2tog over next 2 sc. Rep from * around. Join with sl st to first sc. 42 sts.
28th rnd: Ch 1. 1 sc in each st around. Join with sl st to first sc.
29th rnd: Ch 1. *1 sc in each of next 5 sc. Sc2tog over next 2 sc. Rep from * around. Join with sl st to first sc. 36 sc.
30th rnd: As 28th rnd.
31st rnd: Ch 1. 1 sc in same st as sl st. Sc2tog over next 2 sc. *1 sc in next sc. Sc2tog over next 2 sc. Rep from * around. Join with sl st to first sc. 24 sc.
32nd rnd: As 28th rnd. Stuff body.

Head
1st rnd Ch 1. 1 sc in each sc around. Join with sl st to first sc. 24 sc.
2nd rnd: Ch 1. *1 sc in each of next 3 sc. 2 sc in next sc. Rep from * around. Join with sl st to first sc. 30 sc.
3rd and 4th rnds: Ch 1. 1 sc in each sc around. Join with sl st to first sc.
5th rnd: Ch 1. *1 sc in each of next 4 sc. 2 sc in next sc. Rep from * around. Join with sl st to first sc. 36 sc.

6th to 14th rnds: Ch 1. 1 sc in each st around. Join with sl st to first sc.
15th rnd: Ch 1. Sc2tog over first 2 sc. 1 sc in each of next 15 sc. (Sc2tog over next 2 sc) twice. 1 sc in each sc to last 2 sc. Sc2tog over last 2 sc. Join with sl st to first sc. 32 sts.
16th rnd: Ch 1. (Sc2tog over next 2 sts) 16 times. Join with sl st to first sc. 16 sts.
17th rnd: Ch 1. 1 sc in each st around. Join with sl st to first sc.
18th rnd: Ch 1. (Sc2tog over next 2 sts) 8 times. Join with sl st to first sc. 8 sts. Stuff head.
19th rnd: Ch 1. (Sc2tog over next 2 sts) 4 times. Join with sl st to first sc. 4 sts.
Cut yarn leaving a long end. Thread yarn through last 4 sts and pull tight to close. Secure yarn.

Flower (make 1)
With A, ch 3.
1st rnd: 6 hdc in 3rd ch from hook. Join with sl st to top of first hdc. 6 hdc.
2nd rnd: Ch 2 (does not count as st). 2 hdc in back loop only of each hdc around. Join with sl st to back loop of first hdc.
3rd rnd: As 2nd rnd. 24 hdc.
4th rnd: Ch 2 (does not count as st). *2 hdc in back loop of next hdc. 1 hdc in back loop of each of next 2 hdc. Rep from * around. Join with sl st to both loops of first hdc. 32 hdc.
5th rnd: Ch 1. 1 sc in first hdc.
*Ch 5. Skip next 2 hdc. 1 sc in next hdc. Rep from * to last 3 hdc. Skip next 3 hdc. Ch 5. Join with sl st to first sc.
6th rnd: (Petals). Ch 1. *(1 sc. 1 hdc. 3 dc. 1 hdc. 1 sc) in next ch-5 sp. Rep from * around. Join with sl st to first sc. Fasten off.
Sew Flower to center front of Body, stuffing lightly.

Ears (make 2)
With MC, ch 10.

1st row: (RS). 1 sc in 2nd ch from hook. 1 sc in each ch to end of ch. Turn. 9 sc.

2nd to 4th rows: Ch 1. 1 sc in each sc across. Turn.

5th row: Ch 1. 2 sc in first sc. 1 sc in each sc to last sc. 2 sc in last sc. Turn.

6th to 10th rows: Ch 1. 1 sc in each sc across. Turn.

11th row: As 5th row. 13 sc.

12th to 34th rows: Ch 1. 1 sc in each sc across. Turn.

35th row: Ch 1. Sc2tog over first 2 sc. 1 sc in each sc to last 2 sc. Sc2tog over last 2 sc. Turn. 11 sts.
Rep last row 4 times more. 3 sts. Fasten off.
Fold first row in half and sew to top of Head.

Tail (make 1)
With A, ch 2.

1st rnd: 6 sc in 2nd ch from hook. Join with sl st to first sc. 6 sc.

2nd rnd: Ch 1. 2 sc in each sc around. Join with sl st to first sc. 12 sc.

3rd rnd: Ch 1. (1 sc. 1 dc) in first sc. *(1 dc. 1 sc) in next sc. (1 sc. 1 dc) in next sc. Rep from * to last sc. (1 dc. 1 sc) in last sc. Join with sl st to first sc. Fasten off.
With WS tog, sew tail around, stuffing lightly. Attach tail to back of Body.

FINISHING
Using black yarn, cross-stitch eyes as shown in photo. Using pink yarn, embroider a letter Y shape centered below eyes. Wrap ribbon around Bunny's neck and tie into a bow. Trim ends.

FANTASY flowers blanket

YOU'LL NEED:

YARN
Bernat® Softee Baby
(Solids: 5oz/140g)
(Ombre: 4¼oz/120g)

Main Color (MC)
31415 Candy Baby - 2 balls
Contrast A
30207 Rumba Rose - 1 ball
Contrast B
02001 Pink - 1 ball
Contrast C
30205 Prettiest Pink - 1 ball
Contrast D
30185 Soft Lilac- 1 ball

HOOKS
Size G or 6 (4 mm) crochet hook *or
size to obtain gauge*

MEASUREMENT
Approx 37" [94 cm] square.

GAUGE
17 sc and 18 rows = 4" [10 cm]. *Take time
to check gauge.*

INSTRUCTIONS
Note: When working from Chart, wind
small balls of the colors to be used, one for
each separate area of color in the design.
Start new colors at appropriate points. To
change color, work to last 2 loops on hook.

Draw loop of next color through 2 loops
on hook to complete st and proceed in
next color.

Basic Block
With Color 1, ch 38.
1st row: (RS). 1 sc in 2nd ch from hook and
each ch to end of ch. 37 sc. Turn.
2nd row: Ch 1. Work 2nd row of Chart in
sc, reading row from right to left. Turn.
3rd row: Ch 1. Work 3rd row of Chart in sc,
reading row from left to right. Turn.
Chart is now in position.
Work Chart to end of chart. *Do not* fasten
off at end of last row.

CHART

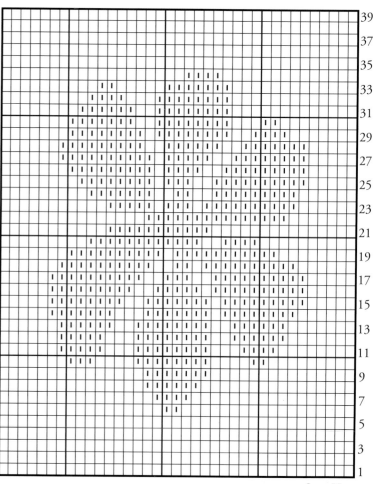

Start Here

Key

☐ = With Color 1, 1 sc.

Ⅰ = With Color 2, 1 sc.

FANTASY flowers blanket

Edging

With Color 1, ch 1. 3 sc in corner. Work 35 sc down left side of Block. 3 sc in corner. Work 1 sc in each of rem 35 loops of foundation ch. 3 sc in corner. Work 35 sc u right side of Block. 3 sc in corner. Work 1 sc in each of next 35 sc across top of Block. Join with sl st to first sc. Fasten off.

Block I (make 4)

Work as given for Basic Block, having A as Color 1 and MC as Color 2.

Block II (make 4)

Work as given for Basic Block, having B as Color 1 and as Color 2.

Block III (make 4)

Work as given for Basic Block, having C as Color 1 and MC as Color 2.

Block IV (make 4)

Work as given for Basic Block, having D as Color 1 and A as Color 2.

FINISHING

Pin Blocks to measurements 9" [23 cm] square, cover with damp cloth, leaving cloth to dry.
Sew blocks tog following Diagram.

Border

With RS of work facing, join MC with sl st in any corner sc. Ch 3 (counts as dc). 2 dc in same sp as sl st. 3 dc in each sc around. Join with sl st to top of ch 3. Fasten off.

BLOCK DIAGRAM

IV	I	II	III
III	IV	I	II
II	III	IV	I
I	II	III	IV